CHESS IS AN EASY GAME

CHESS
is an Easy Game

by

FRED REINFELD

LONDON

LUTTERWORTH PRESS

First published 1961
Second impression 1965
Third impression 1967
Fourth impression 1970

ISBN 0 7188 0145 8

PRINTED IN GREAT BRITAIN BY OFFSET LITHOGRAPHY BY
COMPTON PRINTING LTD., LONDON AND AYLESBURY

CONTENTS

INTRODUCTION

THE title of this book is provocative, and intentionally so. So perhaps it would be well to point out the underlying idea of this title.

To attain true mastery in chess is given to a comparatively small number of gifted, hard-working individuals. But this is not what the ordinary player wants or needs. His ambition is to score creditably against his friends and other opponents who are just ordinary players like himself.

Many players never achieve this rather modest ambition because their approach is purely empirical—they hope to learn by random, undirected experience. This is a method which is almost always doomed to failure.

The right approach, I have concluded after many years of teaching activity, is to familiarize oneself with a concentrated and simplified presentation of the game. *Directed* study of the essentials is the key to success.

As you will soon see, it is very easy to acquire an expert knowledge of chess notation—the simplified description of moves that might well be called the language of chess. By learning this language you open the door to the entrancing world of a very exciting game that trains the mind, calls for concentration, forethought and skill and will provide you with a lifetime of playing pleasure. To make these delights accessible to more and more readers is a chess author's best recompense.

1. THE ELEMENTS

In a game of chess there are two opponents who take turns making moves. One of them ("White") has the white pieces. The other player ("Black") has the black pieces. White always moves first at the beginning of the game.

1. *The Chessboard.*

2. *The Opening Position.*

There are eight horizontal rows, known as "ranks", and eight vertical rows, known as "files". All sixty-four squares are used in the game. Note the white square is always at the lower, right corner.

This is how the forces are placed to start the game. Each player has sixteen chessmen as the game begins.

You will have noticed that there are six different kinds of chessmen shown in Diagram 2. Here are their names:

	WHITE			BLACK	
		one KING			
		one QUEEN			
		two ROOKS			
		two BISHOPS			
		two KNIGHTS			
		eight PAWNS			

7

Here are two important things to keep in mind when you set up the chessmen to begin a game:

(1) The right-hand corner square nearest to White must be a white square.

(2) The two Queens must face each other along the same file, with the White Queen on a white square and the Black Queen on a black square (see Diagram 2). The Kings will also face each other on another file.

The King Bishop is placed on the King Bishop file, next to the King.

The King Knight is placed on the King Knight file, next to the King Bishop.

The King Rook is placed on the King Rook file, next to the King Knight.

The Queen Bishop, Queen Knight and Queen Rook get their names in the same way.

As for the Pawns, each one is named for the piece in front of which it stands on the second rank. Example: the Pawn in front of the Queen is the Queen Pawn.

How the chessmen move

Each of the chessmen has a different way of moving. This variety adds a great deal to the charm of chess, and allows the chessmen to co-operate to produce stunning effects.

The King

3. *How the King moves.*

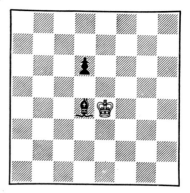

4. *How the King captures.*

The King can move one square in any direction—vertically, horizontally and diagonally to any of the squares marked with a cross. A diagonal is a row of squares of the same colour all extending in the same direction.

The King can capture any hostile chessman on an adjacent square. The King captures by displacement. In Diagram 4 the King can capture the Bishop but not the Pawn.

8

The Queen

The Queen, like the King, can move in any direction. But there is a very important difference—the Queen can keep right on moving until she is blocked by some obstacle to her further progress, such as a friendly chessman. The Queen captures by displacing the hostile chessman it is eliminating.

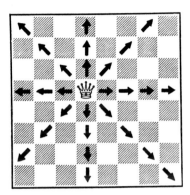
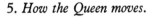

5. How the Queen moves.

6. How the Queen captures.

The Queen can move to any square marked with an arrow. As you can see, the Queen has enormous powers, and you will not be surprised to learn that she is the most powerful piece on the board.

The Queen can capture any one of the three Black chessmen. She can capture the Knight (along the rank); or the Black Bishop (along the file); or the Pawn (along the diagonal).

The Rook

The Rook moves vertically or horizontally, one direction at a time. It is the second most powerful piece on the board.

The Rook can, within its moving range, capture any hostile chessman (see Diagram 8 below). The Rook captures by displacing the hostile chessman it is eliminating. The presence of a friendly chessman along a Rook's line of movement makes it impossible for the Rook to move any further along that line.

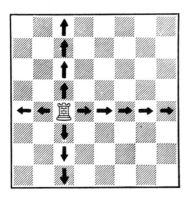

7. *How the Rook moves.*

8. *How the Rook captures.*

The Rook can move to any square marked with an arrow. As you can see, the number of squares available to the Rook is much smaller than the number available to the Queen.

The Rook can capture the Bishop (horizontal move). Or it can capture the Knight (vertical move). But the Rook *cannot* capture the Pawn (diagonal move).

The Bishop

The Bishop moves diagonally, one direction at a time. It is not quite so strong as the Rook.

The Bishop can capture any hostile chessman placed within its moving range (see Diagram 10 below). The Bishop captures by displacement of the hostile chessman which it is eliminating. The presence of a friendly chessman along a Bishop's line of movement makes it impossible for the Bishop to move any further along that line.

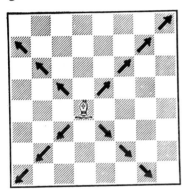

9. *How the Bishop moves.*

10. *How the Bishop captures.*

The Bishop can move to any square marked with an arrow. A Bishop has its greatest scope when placed in the centre.

The Bishop can capture the Rook or the Pawn. The Bishop *cannot* capture the Knight, however, because the Pawn impedes.

The Knight

The Knight's powers are unique in several respects. For example, the Knight is the only piece that can leap over any other chessman. The Knight, unlike the Queen, Rook, or Bishop, has a move of uniform length. Its move is three squares long, and it can take the following forms:

(1) One square forward or backward; then two squares to the right or left.

(2) One square to the right or left; then two squares forward or backward.

These possibilities are shown in Diagrams 11 and 12.

The Knight can capture only on the end-square of its move, displacing the captured chessmen. The Knight cannot capture any chessman that it leaps over. These points are illustrated in Diagrams 13 and 14.

11

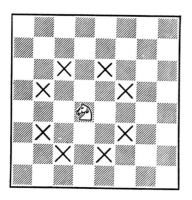

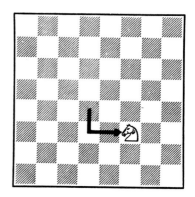

11. *How the Knight moves.*

The Knight can move to any one of the squares marked with a cross.

12. *A typical Knight move.*

The Knight has made one of the moves indicated in Diagram 11.

In mastering the Knight's move, you will find it a big help to remember this feature: every time a Knight moves, it changes the colour of its square. Starting from a white square, it ends up on a black square. On the other hand, if it starts on a black square, it ends on a white square. (Verify this in Diagrams 11 and 12.)

13. *How the Knight captures.*

The Knight can capture only one of these Pawns—namely, the Pawn on the end-square of the Knight's move. The other Pawns are safe from capture.

14. *The completed Knight capture.*

This is the position that results from the only possible Knight capture in Diagram 13. The Knight can never capture the men it leaps over.

The Pawn

The Pawn is the only chessman that can move in only one direction. A White Pawn moves toward the Black side only (Diagrams 15 and 16). A Black Pawn moves toward the White side only (Diagrams 17 and 18). The Pawn moves one square straight ahead unless that square is already occupied by a hostile or friendly man.

15. *The White Pawn moves straight ahead.*

16. *The White Pawn has completed its move.*

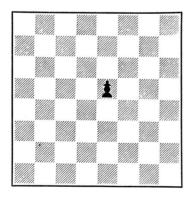

17. *The Black Pawn moves straight ahead.*

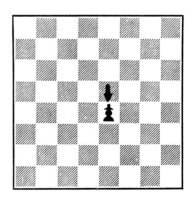

18. *The Black Pawn has completed its move.*

The Pawn has an important option. Each Pawn on its first move—not necessarily the first move in the game—has the choice of advancing one square or two squares. These possibilities are illustrated in Diagrams 19 and 20. For unusual powers of the Pawn see Diagrams 55 to 57.

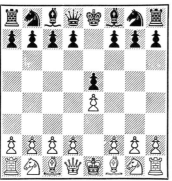

19. *Each King Pawn has advanced two squares.*

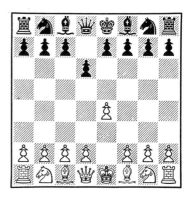

20. *Here Black's Queen Pawn has moved one square; White's Pawn has moved two squares.*

A peculiarity of the Pawn is that, unlike any other chessmen, its capturing method differs from the way it moves. A Pawn captures any hostile unit that is diagonally in front of it, to the left or right.

21. *No capture possible.*

Neither Pawn can capture the other. The Pawns merely block each other.

22. *A choice of captures.*

The White Pawn can capture the Black Queen or the Black Knight.

14

23. *The Pawn can capture the Bishop.*

24. *The Pawn has captured the Bishop.*

CHECK AND CHECKMATE

Though the King is not the strongest piece in chess, it is the most important piece.

Basically, you win a game of chess by attacking the hostile King until it has no escape from capture. Such a situation is known as "Checkmate". (Actually the King is never captured; the fact that the King is attacked and cannot escape is what establishes checkmate.)

An attack on the King is called a "check". If the King can escape from attack, he does so, and the game goes on. If he cannot escape from attack, then he is checkmated, and the game is over. The player who has brought about the checkmate has won the game.

There are three ways of getting out of check:

(1) Capture the hostile man that is giving check.

(2) Move the King off the line of attack. Naturally, you are not permitted to move the King to a square commanded by some other hostile man.

(3) Place one of your own men on the line of attack between your King and the hostile man that is giving check.

These methods are illustrated in Diagrams 25 to 28.

15

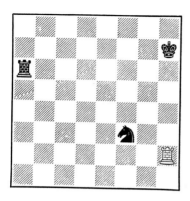

25. *White's Rook is giving check.*
Black's King is in check.

26. *Black is out of check.*
The Black Knight has captured the White Rook.

27. *Black is out of check.*
Black has moved his King off the line of attack. This is the second method.

28. *Black is out of check.*
Black has interposed his Rook on the line of attack. This is the third method.

16

To understand the nature of checkmate, you must keep in mind that a King can never move to a square which is in the capturing range of a hostile man.

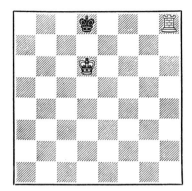

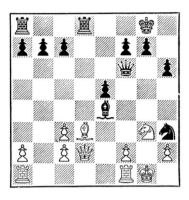

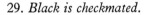

29. *Black is checkmated.*

White's Rook is checking the Black King. Horizontal King moves are useless, as the King remains on the line of attack. Other King moves are impossible as they would bring the Black King inside the capturing range of the White King. Finally, White's Rook cannot be captured.

30. *White is checkmated.*

Black's Knight is checking White's King. White cannot capture the Knight. White cannot interpose (one can never interpose to a Knight check). And the White King cannot move into the Black Bishop's capturing range.

B

Discovered Check

Generally a piece gives check by moving to the proper square for that purpose. In the case of a discovered ("uncovered") check, the checking piece stands still while one of its colleagues moves off the line of attack, allowing the hitherto hidden piece to give check.

This is illustrated in Diagram 31, where White's Queen need not move to give check. This is accomplished by advancing the Pawn.

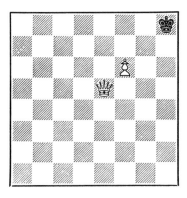

31. *The Pawn advances.*

White moves his Pawn in order to give a discovered check with his Queen, which remains unmoved.

32. *Discovered check.*

Black's King is in check, despite the fact that the White Queen has not moved.

Double Check

The double check is a special and particularly formidable kind of discovered check.

What happens in a double check is that the piece that uncovers the line of attack also gives check as it moves off. Thus in Diagram 33 the Bishop will move and open up the Queen's line of attack. But in addition, the Bishop itself will also give check.

In the case of a simple discovered check, the defender theoretically has the choice of the three possible ways of answering a check—capturing the checking man, moving the King out of check, or interposing on the line of attack. Against a double check, there is only one possible defence—moving the King out of both lines of attack.

18

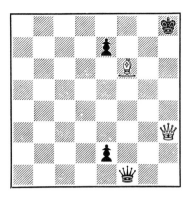

33. *The Bishop moves.*

White will move his Bishop to open the Queen's line of attack. But the Bishop will also give check.

34. *Double Check.*

Both White's Queen and his Bishop are giving check. Black cannot capture the Bishop or Queen.

CASTLING

We have learned that the outcome of a game of chess centres about the fate of the King. We saw that the King himself does not have very much power. This all-important piece therefore requires the most careful shielding to keep it out of harm's way.

One of the most effective devices to guard the King's safety is the process known as "castling". This is a special move performed by the King and a Rook. It can be played only once during the course of a game, and it is the only move in chess in which two different pieces take part—with both moves counting as a single move. Castling with the King Rook is known as "King-side castling". Castling with the Queen Rook is "Queen-side castling".

One basic requirement for castling is that the squares between the King and his castling Rook are empty.

19

King-side Castling

In King-side castling (Diagram 35), White moves his King two squares to the right. He then places his King Rook directly to the left of the King's new position (Diagram 36).

35. *Before King-side castling.*
White is about to castle.

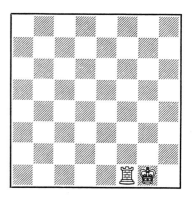

36. *After King-side castling.*
White has castled.

As for Black (Diagram 37), he moves his King two squares to his left. He then places his King Rook directly to the right of the King's new position (Diagram 38).

37. *Before King-side castling.*
Black is about to castle.

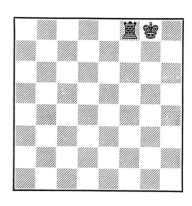

38. *After King-side castling.*
Black has castled.

Queen-side Castling

To castle on the Queen-side (Diagram 39), White moves his King two squares to the left. He then places his Queen Rook directly to the right of his King's new position (Diagram 40).

39. *Before Queen-side castling.*
White is about to castle.

40. *After Queen-side castling.*
White has castled.

When Black castles on the Queen-side (Diagram 41) he moves his King two squares to his right. He then places his Queen Rook directly to the left of his King's new position (Diagram 42).

41. *Before Queen-side castling.*
Black is about to castle.

42. *After Queen-side castling.*
Black has castled.

Restrictions on Castling

There are two kinds of restrictions on castling; some of these hold good for the whole game, while others may not apply later on in the game.

There are two kinds of permanent restrictions. If the King has already moved (Diagram 43), then castling is permanently impossible.

If the Rook desired for castling has already moved (Diagram 44), castling with that Rook is impossible.

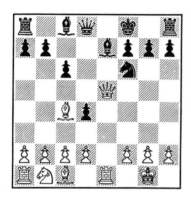

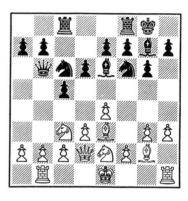

43. *Black can never castle.*

Black has moved his King; hence castling is permanently barred.

44. *White cannot castle Queen-side.*

However, he can castle with his unmoved King Rook.

Now we turn to the castling restrictions that are temporary. By this we mean that if the restrictive condition disappears, it will then be possible to castle.

Castling is temporarily impossible if all the squares between King and Rook are not vacant (Diagram 45).

Castling is temporarily impossible for a King that is in check (Diagram 46). If the King gets out of check without moving, castling will then become feasible.

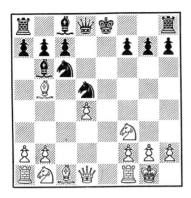

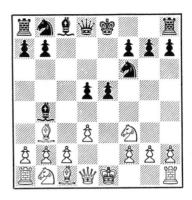

45. *Black is temporarily unable to castle Queen-side.*

He can, however, castle King-side if he wishes.

46. *White is temporarily unable to castle because his King is in check.*

Castling is temporarily impossible if a King, in order to castle, would have to pass over a square controlled by an enemy unit (Diagram 47).

And of course, castling is temporarily impossible if it would land the King on a square controlled by an enemy unit (Diagram 48).

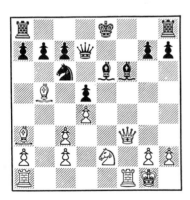

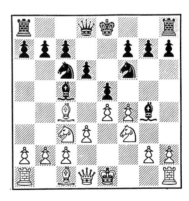

47. *Black is temporarily unable to castle on the King-side.*

The black square over which the King has to pass is controlled by the White Queen Bishop.

48. *White is temporarily unable to castle.*

Castling would land his King on a square commanded by Black's King Bishop.

RELATIVE VALUE OF THE CHESS FORCES

Each unit on the chessboard has a value which is different from the values of other units. How can you know whether you are giving up a more valuable unit in return for capturing a less valuable one? Or, how can you know whether you are gaining a hostile unit of greater value than the unit you are giving up in exchange?

There is a common-sense solution to this problem. The Pawn is the least valuable of all the various units, so we give it an arbitrary value. Then we express the values of the other units in terms of that value.

So, to begin with, we say the Pawn is worth one point. This gives us the following table of values:

Queen	9 points
Rook	5 points
Bishop	3 points
Knight	3 points
Pawn	1 point

We cannot assign any value to the King since the outcome of the game hinges on his preservation!

When we study this table we can derive some valuable conclusions:

The Queen is the strongest and most valuable of the pieces (always excepting the King, of course).

A Bishop and a Knight are of equal value. This means you can readily give up a Bishop in exchange for a hostile Knight; or you can give up a Knight in exchange for a hostile Bishop.

A Rook is definitely worth more than a Bishop or Knight. Winning your opponent's Rook in return for a "minor piece" (Bishop or Knight of your own) is known as "winning the Exchange". Losing your Rook in return for a hostile minor piece is "losing the Exchange".

A minor piece plus two Pawns is roughly the equivalent of a Rook.

A Rook and two Pawns are roughly the equivalent of two minor pieces.

The Pawn is the least valuable of the units—but don't despise the "lowly" Pawn. There are special situations in which you can convert a Pawn into a Queen. This is our next subject to be discussed.

24

OTHER POWERS OF THE PAWN

In the original treatment of the Pawn's powers, two points were left for later discussion. Let us take them up at this time.

Pawn Promotion

When a Pawn reaches the eighth rank—that is to say, the last square in a file—it is promoted to a higher rank. It can and must be converted into a Queen or Rook or Bishop or Knight at the player's option. Generally a new Queen is his choice, as this piece is the strongest on the board, but there is no limitation on the player's choice. For example, even if he still has his original Queen he is not debarred from promoting to a second Queen.

The advance of a Pawn to the eighth rank and its replacement by a new piece of the same colour are all considered to comprise a single move. Thereafter the newly promoted piece must wait for the opponent's reply before making its first move.

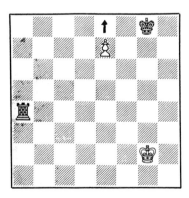

49. *White promotes his Pawn.*

White advances his Pawn to the eighth rank, replacing it with a White Queen.

50. *The new Queen in action.*

White's new Queen gives check and also attacks Black's Rook, winning the Rook next move.

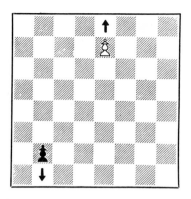

51. Both players obtain new Queens.

First White advances his Pawn and obtains a new Queen. Then Black advances his Pawn and likewise obtains a new Queen.

52. Both players have new Queens.

Each player has advanced a Pawn to the last rank and obtained a new Queen. Note that the Pawns "queen" at opposite ends of the board.

53. Black's King must move.

In moving, Black can no longer guard his Bishop Pawn. His King retreats, and the Pawn falls.

54. Black loses his last Pawn.

White will capture the Black Pawn. His own Pawn will then be free to advance.

It is not surprising that the queening of a Pawn is often the means of winning a game. Suppose that in the position of Diagram 53 White had no Pawn left. In

26

that case he could not win, as King and Bishop cannot force checkmate. However, as matters stand, he can win the Black Pawns, after which his remaining Pawn, escorted by King and Bishop, advances to the queening square. Then, having obtained a new Queen, he forces checkmate quickly and easily. Thus the seemingly insignificant Pawn is the key to victory.

Very often when one of the players has obtained a considerable advantage ("plus") in material and checkmate is a foregone conclusion, his opponent will resign—concede defeat—instead of playing out the dismal interval that will elapse before checkmate takes place.

Pawn Captures En Passant ("In Passing")

This is an unusual form of capture which is possible only when four specific conditions exist:
(1) The Pawn that does the capturing must be on its fifth rank.
(2) The hostile Pawn that is destined to be captured must be on an adjacent file and on its original rank (Diagram 55).
(3) It is the opponent's turn to move and he advances his Pawn two squares (Diagram 56).
(4) The hostile Pawn, having advanced two squares, can be captured as if it had advanced only one square (Diagram 57).

55. En passant capture.

First stage: the Pawns are on adjacent files. One Pawn is on its fifth rank, the other Pawn is on its second rank.

56. *En passant capture.*

Second stage: the Black Pawn advances two squares.

57. *En passant capture.*

Final stage: the White Pawn captures the Black Pawn en passant.

While capturing in passing is purely optional, the capture, if it is to be played at all, must come on the immediate reply to the two-square advance of the hostile Pawn. If not exercised at once, the option lapses.

If capturing in passing is the only way to answer a check to one's King, then the capture is compulsory. On the other hand, if capturing in passing would expose one's King to attack, then such capture is impossible.

HOW TO READ CHESS MOVES

There are several systems for recording chess moves. They are all based on the same principle: each chessman and each square must have a definite name. These names are derived from the opening position (Diagram 58).

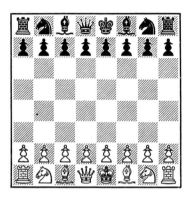

58. *The opening position.*

59. *The Files.*

QUEEN-ROOK'S FILE | QUEEN-KNIGHT'S FILE | QUEEN-BISHOP'S FILE | QUEEN'S FILE | KING'S FILE | KING-BISHOP'S FILE | KING-KNIGHT'S FILE | KING-ROOK'S FILE

The names of the pieces, reading from left to right, appear below. The Pawns get their names from the pieces in front of which they are placed (for example, Queen Pawn in front of the Queen, etc.). Note the abbreviations commonly used.

The files are named for the pieces (and the accompanying Pawns) that are placed on them at the beginning of the game. These names are permanent, even though the position of the identifying pieces and Pawns will change during the game.

Names of the Pieces

Queen Rook (QR)

Queen Knight (QKt)

Queen Bishop (QB)

Queen (Q)

King (K)

King Bishop (KB)

King Knight (KKt)

King Rook (KR)

Names of the Corresponding Pawns

Queen Rook Pawn (QRP)

Queen Knight Pawn (QKtP)

Queen Bishop Pawn (QBP)

Queen Pawn (QP)

King Pawn (KP)

King Bishop Pawn (KBP)

King Knight Pawn (KKtP)

King Rook Pawn (KRP)

The ranks are the horizontal rows that are numbered by each player from *his* side of the board (Diagrams 60 and 61).

8 WHITE'S EIGHTH RANK
7
6
5
4
3
2
1 WHITE'S   FIRST   RANK

1 BLACK'S   FIRST   RANK
2
3
4
5
6
7
8 BLACK'S EIGHTH RANK

60. *The ranks from White's side.*

The recording of White's moves is based on his numbering of the ranks as shown above.

61. *The ranks from Black's side.*

The recording of Black's moves is based on his numbering of the ranks as shown above.

Now that we know the names of all the files (Diagram 59) and the numbers of all the ranks (Diagrams 60 and 61), we have all the information we need for recording moves.

Here is the most important point to remember: each rank has two numbers—White's number and Black's number. In Diagram 61 White's second rank becomes Black's seventh rank, for example. Also, you can see that each square has to have two names—one from White's side of the board and one from Black's side of the board.

Now when White is recording his moves, he uses the White numbering of the ranks (Diagram 60). When Black is recording *his* moves, he uses the Black numbering of the ranks.

As you can see from Diagram 62, the name of any square is a combination of the file and rank on which it stands. For example, the square on which the King stands is King 1 (K1), or first square on the King file. The square on which the King Pawn stands is King 2 (K2), or the second square in the King file.

In Diagram 62 the name at the bottom of each square is White's name for that square and it is used to record White moves. The upside-down name of each square is Black's name for that square, and is used to record Black moves.

BLACK

QR8	QKt8	QB8	Q8	K8	KB8	KKt8	KR8
QR7	QKt7	QB7	Q7	K7	KB7	KKt7	KR7
QR6	QKt6	QB6	Q6	K6	KB6	KKt6	KR6
QR5	QKt5	QB5	Q5	K5	KB5	KKt5	KR5
QR4	QKt4	QB4	Q4	K4	KB4	KKt4	KR4
QR3	QKt3	QB3	Q3	K3	KB3	KKt3	KR3
QR2	QKt2	QB2	Q2	K2	KB2	KKt2	KR2
QR1	QKt1	QB1	Q1	K1	KB1	KKt1	KR1

WHITE

62. *The names of the squares.*

To record a move, we write down the name of the unit that is making the move, add a dash and then the name of the square to which it has moved. For example, if White moves his King Pawn two squares he writes, "P—K4". If Black replies by advancing *his* King Pawn two squares he also writes, "P—K4". (This gives us the position of Diagram 63.)

In an ordinary game score (also known as the "text" of the game), the moves are listed in two columns, with White's moves in the left column and Black's moves in the right column. In addition the moves are numbered, so that you can follow the correct order of the moves.

31

To save time, we use abbreviations and short-cut symbols for the moves. Here are the most important ones:

King	K	discovered check	dis ch
Queen	Q	double check	dbl ch
Rook	R	*en passant* (in passing)	*e.p.*
Bishop	B		
Knight	Kt	a good move	!
Pawn	P	a very good move	!!
captures	×	a bad move	?
moves to	—	a very bad move	??
check	ch	from or at	/

A SAMPLE GAME

If you are eager to become a good player—and who isn't?—you will benefit enormously from studying chess books. It is easy to do once you are familiar with the recording of chess moves. Here is a short, instructive game which has the additional virtue of illustrating dynamic winning tactics.

	WHITE	BLACK
1	P—K4	P—K4
2	Kt—KB3	Kt—KB3
3	Kt×P	Kt—B3

32

4	Kt×Kt	QP×Kt
5	P—Q3	B—QB4
6	B—Kt5	Kt×P!!
7	B×Q	B×Pch
8	K—K2	B—KKt5 mate

Since the recording of moves is still a novel experience to you, we will follow the course of the game in slow motion through a detailed series of diagrams. To begin, set up the forces on your chessboard in the opening position (Diagram 58) and make each recorded move. If any of the moves puzzle you, consult Diagram 62 for the names of the squares.

The game starts with White playing 1 P—K4 and Black replying 1 . . . P—K4. This gives us the situation in Diagram 63.

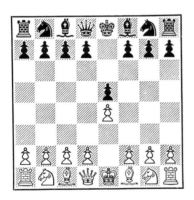

63. *Play continues:*

	WHITE	BLACK
2	Kt—KB3	Kt—KB3
3	Kt×P	Kt—B3
4	Kt×Kt	QP×Kt

See Diagram 64.

64. *Play continues:*

	WHITE	BLACK
5	P—Q3	B—QB4
6	B—Kt5	Kt×P!!

On the face of it, a terrible blunder.

See Diagram 65.

33

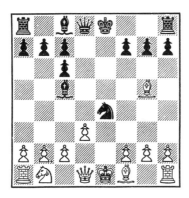 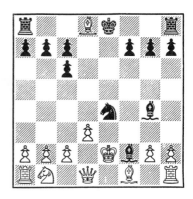

65. *Play continues:*		66. *Final position:*

<table>
<tr><td colspan="2">WHITE   BLACK</td></tr>
</table>

	WHITE	BLACK
7	B×Q	B×Pch
8	K—K2	B—KKt5mate

See Diagram 66.

66. *Final position:*

White's King has no escape. Black's brilliant Queen sacrifice resulted in a very quick checkmate.

We have seen that the basic method of winning a game of chess is to checkmate the opposing King. A common way of leading up to this is to gain material—to win your opponent's pieces or to capture more valuable ones in exchange for less valuable pieces of your own. Another way of leading up to victory is to promote one of your Pawns to a new Queen. Very often when one player is considerably ahead in material, his outnumbered opponent simply "resigns"—he formally admits defeat. The game is over, just as if he had been checkmated. Not all games, however, end with checkmate or resignation. Some are "drawn"—they end with victory for neither side.

DRAWN GAMES

A draw is a game which ends with honours even—each side scores a half-point. Here are the ways in which such a result may come about.

Drawing Methods
A draw can be declared by mutual agreement of the players.

34

Either player can claim a draw if fifty moves have been made by each player without a capture or Pawn move having been made. (This is likely to arise only at a very advanced, highly simplified stage of the game.)

A player can claim a draw if he is on the point of making a move that would result for the third time in the same position.

There are other drawing possibilities that require more detailed description.

Inadequate Checkmating Material

A player may be ahead in material but his margin of advantage may not be enough to force checkmate. It is impossible, for example, to force checkmate in endings with King and Bishop against King, or King and Knight against King (See Diagram 67), or even with King and two Knights against King.

Draw by Perpetual Check

This self-explanatory term applies to situations in which a player has the power to give an endless series of checks. It is a device that makes it possible to convert an otherwise surely lost game into a forced draw. See Diagram 68, in which White, although he is a long way behind in material, is able to force a draw.

67. Drawn position.

68. Perpetual check.

White's King can never be cornered, as some means of escape will always be available. The ending of King and Bishop against King is equally futile.

WHITE	BLACK
1 Q—K8ch	K—R2
2 Q—R5ch	K—Kt1
3 Q—K8ch	K—R2
4 Q—R5ch etc.	

Draw by Stalemate

This method of causing a drawn game has to be distinguished very carefully from checkmate. In the case of checkmate, the King is attacked (in check) and has no legal move.

In the case of stalemate, the following conditions have to be fulfilled:

(1) The player who claims stalemate has to be on the move, i.e. his move next.

(2) His King must *not* be in check.

(3) The only moves left to him would place his King inside the capturing range of some hostile unit.

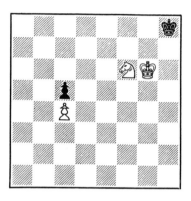

69. Stalemate.

Black (to move) is stalemated. Any move of the Black King would bring him inside the capturing range of White's Queen.

70. Stalemate.

Black (to move) is stalemated. His Pawn cannot move and any move of his King would bring him inside the capturing range of White's King or Knight.

2. WINNING OBJECTIVES

Forcing checkmate is always our basic goal in a game of chess. Meanwhile, our immediate aims are: winning material; checks; Pawn promotion; and threats. Each of these may be a step on the way to checkmate.

Checkmate Patterns

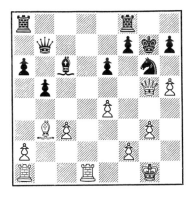

71. *Mate on King Knight 7.*

72. *Mate on the long diagonal.*

White to move. Ordinarily White's proper play would be P×Kt. Here, however, he has a stronger move:

WHITE	BLACK
1 P—R6ch!	K moves
2 Q—B6	. . . . .

Black is helpless against 3 Q—Kt7 mate.

Black to move. Based on the power of his Bishop on the long diagonal, this brilliant sacrifice is conclusive:

WHITE	BLACK
1	R×P!
2 K×R	Q—R3ch
3 K—Kt1	Q—R8 mate

73. *Mating attack against King Rook* 7.

74. *Smothered mate.*

White to move.

WHITE	BLACK
1 B—R7ch	K—R1
2 B—Kt6 dis ch!	K—Kt1
3 Q—R7ch	K—B1
4 Q×P mate	

This is a very common form of attack, with many applications in actual play.

White to move.

WHITE	BLACK
1 Q—Q5ch	K—R1
(*or* 1	K—B1;
and then 2 Q—B7 mate.)	
2 Kt—B7ch	K—Kt1
3 Kt—R6 dbl ch!	K—R1
4 Q—Kt8ch!!	R×Q
5 Kt—B7 mate	

This spectacular mating technique leads to a pleasing finish.

Checkmate Threats Can Win Material

Even if your opponent can parry it, a checkmate threat may still lead to decisive material gains. Diagrams 75 and 76 illustrate the point effectively.

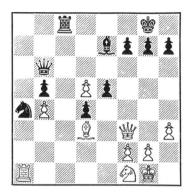

75. *Checkmate menace.*

White to move.

WHITE	BLACK
1 Q—B5!	.....

White threatens Q×RPch followed by Q—R8 mate, and he attacks Black's Rook at the same time.

| 1 ..... | P—Kt3 |

Black can stop the mate but he cannot save his Rook.

  2 Q×Rch and wins.

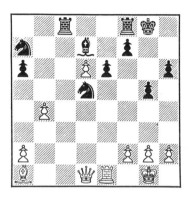

76. *Checkmate menace.*

White to move.

WHITE	BLACK
1 Q—Q4!	.....

White threatens Q—Kt7 mate or Q—R8 mate and attacks Black's Knight at Queen Rook 7 as well.

| 1 ..... | P—B3 |

Black stops the mate but he cannot parry the other threat.

  2 Q×Kt/R7 and wins.

39

Checks Win Material

Many a check has a secondary purpose—to attack another unit in addition to the hostile King. This is shown in Diagrams 77 and 78.

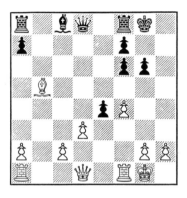

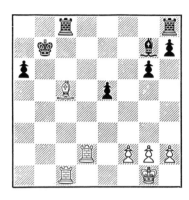

77. *A versatile check.* Black to move.

78. *Two versatile checks.* White to move.

WHITE	BLACK
1	Q—Kt3ch

This check wins White's Bishop, as White must concentrate on getting out of check. This kind of *double attack* occurs very frequently.

WHITE	BLACK
1 R—Q7ch	R—B2

Else White captures the Bishop.

2 R×Rch	K×R
3 B—B8 dis ch	......

White wins the Bishop.

40

Pawn Promotion Wins Material

The conversion of a Pawn into a unit of higher value, when successfully executed, will often win material. See Diagrams 79 and 80.

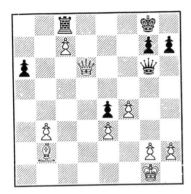 

79. *The Queen Bishop Pawn queens.*

White to move.

WHITE	BLACK
1 Q—Q7!	R—B1

If Black defends the attacked Rook with 1 ...... Q—K1 White replies 2 Q×P mate.

| 2 P—B8/Q | R×Q |

Black has no choice.

3 Q×Rch and wins

80. *The Queen Knight Pawn queens.*

White to move.

WHITE	BLACK
1	R—R8

Black threatens 2 ...... R×R; 3 Q×R, P—Kt8/Q with a whole Queen ahead.

| 2 R—Kt1 | R×R |
| 3 Q×R | Kt—B6 and wins |

Black gets a new Queen.

41

Threats Win Material

There are many kinds of threats which win material because your opponent cannot defend himself against every possibility. The point is effectively made in Diagrams 81 and 82.

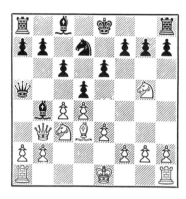

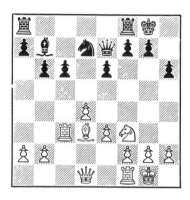

81. *Black wins by a double attack.*

82. *The Queen Bishop Pawn is the target.*

Black to move.

WHITE	BLACK
1	P×P!

This is really a triple attack! The Pawn capture attacks White's Queen and Bishop—and also his advanced Knight as well.

| 2 B×BP | B×Ktch! |

Here 2 ...... Q×Kt? is wrong because of 3 Q×B.

| 3 P×B | Q×Kt and wins. |

White to move.

WHITE	BLACK
1 B—K4!	KR—B1

White threatened 2 B×P. Now he simply keeps renewing the threat.

2 Q—B2	Q—Q3
3 KR—B1	Kt—Kt1
4 Kt—K5	......

This finally wins the Queen Bishop Pawn, as Black has run out of defensive resources.

3. WINNING METHODS

As we have seen in the previous section, it is important to know our basic winning objectives. But this is not the whole story: we also have to be familiar with winning techniques and able to recognize winning possibilities.

Exposed King

This is one of the best guides we have for the progress of a winning attack. Sometimes the hostile King is approachable through a line of attack, or because he is not securely guarded by his pieces. See Diagrams 83 and 84.

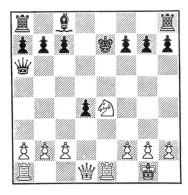

83. *A deadly discovered check.*

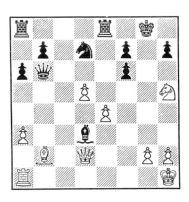

84. *Unavoidable mate.*

White to move. The presence of Black's King on an open file proves fatal.

WHITE	BLACK
1 Kt—B5 dis ch	.....

Thanks to the exposed position of Black's King, White wins his Queen for a mere Knight.

White to move. Black's King Knight Pawn has captured on his King Bishop 3, opening up a gaping hole in his castled position. Therefore:

WHITE	BLACK
1 Q—R6	......

Black cannot prevent Q—Kt7 mate.

Open Lines

Open lines enormously increase the mobility of your forces, making it possible for them to manoeuvre more effectively. And when one or more of these open lines lead to the vicinity of the hostile King, it may well be that you have the makings of a violent, quickly decisive attack. See Diagrams 85 and 86.

85. *The open Queen Knight file.*

86. *The open King Rook file.*

Black to move. Black wins on the spot with:

WHITE	BLACK
1	Q—Kt3!!

This threatens ...... Q×P mate and also ...... Q×B ch.

| 2 B×Q | Kt—K7 mate |

A deadly double check.

White to move. The open file is White's highway to victory. In fact, he has a forced mate.

WHITE	BLACK
1 R—R8 ch	K—B2
2 Q×Kt ch!	K×Q
3 R/R1—R7 mate	

Preponderance of Pieces

If you have more attacking units than your opponent has available for defence, you will succeed in your aim whatever it may be, but even material equality becomes unimportant when you possess a concentration of force on a vulnerable point. See Diagrams 87 and 88.

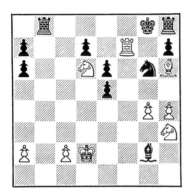

87. *Windmill checks.*

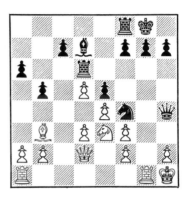

88. *Queen sacrifice.*

White to move. The co-operation of his Rook, Bishop and Knight is something to marvel at.

	WHITE	BLACK
1	R—Kt7ch	K—B1
2	R×QP dis ch	K—Kt1
3	R—KKt7 ch	K—B1
4	R—QKt7 dis ch	K—Kt1
5	R×Rch	Kt—B1
6	R×Kt mate	

Black to move. He can bring a heavy concentration of forces to bear on the hostile King, while White's forces are shut off from the defence.

	WHITE	BLACK
1	......	Q×RPch!!
	Beautiful play.	
2	K×Q	R—R3ch
3	K—Kt3	R—R6 mate

The Fork

This simultaneous attack on two hostile units is perhaps the deadliest attack in chess. When this attack operates in different directions, it is particularly likely to be overlooked by inexperienced players. This is particularly true of the Knight fork—the most common, and most insidious, of the forks. See Diagrams 89 to 91.

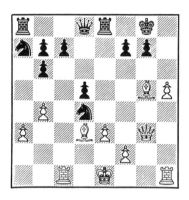

89. *A Knight fork.*

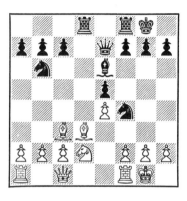

90. *Prepared Knight fork.*

Black to move. A sham Queen sacrifice is justified by the resulting Knight fork.

WHITE	BLACK
1	Q × B!
2 Q × Q	Kt—B6ch

This Knight fork is followed by 3 ...... Kt × Q, leaving Black a piece ahead.

Black to move. He wants to play the deadly forking move ...... Kt—K7ch, winning White's Queen; but White's Bishop on Queen 3 foils him; so:

WHITE	BLACK
1	R × B!
2 P × R	Kt—K7ch

Black wins the White Queen.

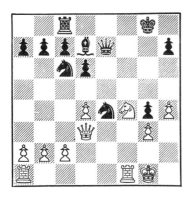

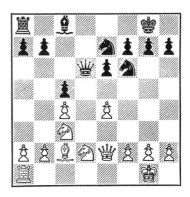

91. *An elaborately prepared Knight fork.*

White to move.

WHITE	BLACK
1 Kt—Q5!	Q—K3
2 Q×Kt!	Q×Q
3 Kt—B6ch	.....

White continues with 4 Kt×Q, remaining with a substantial advantage in material.

92. *A Pawn fork.*

White to move. This type of attack is dreaded because the attacker's investment is so small.

WHITE	BLACK
1 P—K5	.....

White attacks two Black pieces, thereby forcing the win of a piece.

The Pin

This is the most common of all attacking methods in chess. It is an attack on two units standing on a file, rank or diagonal. There is a direct attack on the nearest hostile piece—the pinned piece—on the line of attack. There is a contingent attack on the second hostile unit which is screened from attack by the pinned piece. In Diagram 93 Black's King Bishop Pawn is pinned, as it screens Black's King from attack. In Diagram 94 Black's Knight at his King Bishop 2 is pinned, again screening the Black King from attack.

The screened piece is generally one of very high value—King or Queen. (See Diagrams 93 to 96.) When the King is the screened piece—as in Diagram 93—the pinned unit cannot budge; for any such move would expose its King to check. If any piece but the King is being screened, it can be exposed to attack by a move of the pinned unit; but this is undesirable because of the loss of material involved.

47

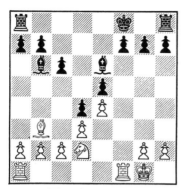

93. *The pin wins a piece.*

White to move.

WHITE	BLACK
1 B×B	.....

White wins a clear piece, as Black cannot recapture, because his King Bishop Pawn is pinned by White's King Rook. This is a very common pattern.

95. *Fork plus pin.*

Black to move. First he pins White's Queen.

WHITE	BLACK
1	B—KKt5!
2 Q×B	Kt—K6ch!

This Knight fork wins the White Queen because his Queen Pawn is pinned.

94. *The pin leads to mate.*

White to move.

WHITE	BLACK
1 R×Kt!	P×R
2 B—R8!	.....

Black cannot prevent Q—Kt7 mate, as ..... K×B or ..... Kt×B is impossible.

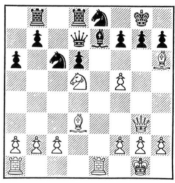

96. *Fork plus pin.*

White to move. Note how White exploits his pin on Black's King Knight Pawn.

WHITE	BLACK
1 R×B!	Kt×R
2 Kt—B6ch!	Kt×Kt
3 Q×KtP mate	

Very cleverly played.

Discovered Attack

This is another attacking device which is exceptionally strong against inexperienced players. It comprises two simultaneous attacks in this manner: a piece makes a powerful attack without moving, as the result of an uncovering move by one of its colleagues which is likewise following up an aggressive idea.

For example, in Diagram 97 White's Knight at Queen 4 attacks Black's Queen and, in so doing, uncovers an attack by White's Queen on one of the Black Knights. Result: White wins a piece, as Black must save his Queen.

In Diagram 98 White gives check with a Bishop and in the process he uncovers an attack by his Queen on Black's unguarded Queen. Here White wins the Black Queen as Black must get out of check.

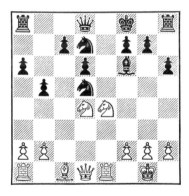 

97. *Discovered attack by a White Knight.*

White to move.

	WHITE	BLACK
1	Kt—B6!	Q moves
2	Q × Kt and wins	

98. *Discovered attack by a White Bishop.*

White to move.

	WHITE	BLACK
1	B × Pch!	K × B
2	Q × Q and wins	

D

Unexpected Captures

The average player constantly overlooks possible captures—either of his own pieces, or the enemy's. Missing these opportunities often leads to disaster. By the same token, taking advantage of them is frequently the way to win. See Diagrams 99 and 100.

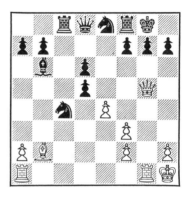

99. *All is not lost.*

Black to move. At first glance he seems hopelessly lost because of White's threatened Q × KtP mate. Yet, if he is alert, Black can completely turn the tables.

WHITE	BLACK
1	Q × Rch!

White resigns, for now Black's King Knight Pawn is no longer pinned, permitting 2 ...... P × Q in reply to 2 K × Q.

100. *Sudden checkmate.*

White to move. Obviously White has a very powerful game on the open King Knight file, but how many players could see the following fine finish:

WHITE	BLACK
1 Q × KtPch!!	Kt × Q
2 R × Ktch	K—R1
3 R—Kt8 dbl ch!!	K × R
4 R—KKt1ch	Q—Kt4
5 R × Q mate	

A glorious finish.

Exploiting Inferior Moves

It is the hallmark of a good player that he immediately seizes on hostile weaknesses. In the following section we shall examine in some detail the ways in which such weaknesses are created. But here we can see the fatal consequences of two types of weak play.

One of these is a substantial loss of time in the opening because of ill-considered Pawn-grabbing expeditions. This is illustrated in Diagram 101, where we have a situation in which White has a significant advantage in open lines and actively functioning pieces. These outweigh by far the two measly Pawns that Black has confiscated.

Diagram 102 illustrates still another faulty type of play in the opening—sending the Queen on distant excursions far from the real scene of action. The punishment is swift and crushing.

101. *Mobility wins.*

White to move.

WHITE	BLACK
1 Q×Pch!!	Resigns

For 1 . . . . . . Kt×Q allows 2 B×P mate.

102. *Checkmate.*

Black to move.

WHITE	BLACK
1	Kt×Pch
2 K—K2	Q—Q6 mate

White's Queen was missed.

51

4. THE OPENING

Our basic task in the opening stage of any game is to bring out our pieces—"develop" them. As long as they are on their original squares they are useless. Development of the pieces gives them real scope and enables them to work efficiently for attack, defence, and manoeuvring—gradual improvement of one's position.

There are twenty possible choices for the first move. Which is the best one to play?

Always start with 1 P—K4

Long experience has shown that 1 P—K4 is the best opening move for inexperienced players. One of the virtues of this move is that it helps to control important centre squares. This follows from the fact that your opponent cannot afford to place his pieces on squares which are controlled by your Pawns.

This brings us to another vital point. A piece has more scope on a centre square or near the centre squares than anywhere else on the board. If 1 P—K4 prevents enemy pieces from occupying this desirable sector, this reinforces our confidence in the value of 1 P—K4.

Some of the points discussed thus far are illustrated in Diagram 103. This position arises from the following moves:

WHITE	BLACK
1 P—K4	Kt—KR3?

This is bad as Black is developing his Knight *away* from the centre.

| 2 P—Q4 | . . . |

Excellent. White secures more control of the centre squares, and meanwhile he has opened the diagonals of both Bishops. He has splendid prospects for future development.

| 2. . . . | Kt—R3? |

Worse and worse. He has continued to neglect the centre.

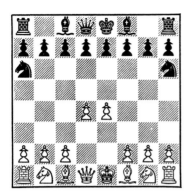

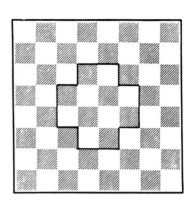

103. *Neglected centre.*

(after 2 . . . . . . Kt—R3)

White has already achieved a significant advantage. Thanks to his control of the centre he will command more of the board and get a more efficient development as the opening unfolds.

104. *The vital centre.*

The squares inside the heavily marked border make up the centre. Comparing this with Diagram 103, we can see that Black's badly developed Knights have virtually no contact with the centre.

To sum up the situation in Diagram 103, we can conclude that even as early as the second move, Black has a strategically lost game!

Avoid Self-blocking Moves

There is no surer way to hamper the development process than to make moves with Pawns or pieces that block some indicated future development. Diagrams 105 and 106 are cases in point.

Diagram 105 arises from this sequence: White plays 1 P—K4, and Black replies 1 . . . P—K4. So far, so good. But now White goes astray with 2 Kt—K2?—a bad move on two counts, as explained in the caption to Diagram 105.

Now consider this sequence:

WHITE	BLACK
1 P—K4	P—K4
2 Kt—KB3	Kt—QB3

The Knight moves on both sides are excellent. Now White fares best with another developing move, say 3 B—Kt5 or 3 B—B4. Instead there follows:

3 P—B3	P—Q4!

53

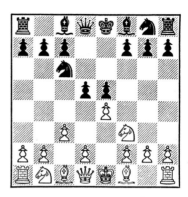

105. *Self-blocking Knight move.*

(after 2 Kt—K2)

106. *Self-blocking Pawn move.*

(after 3 . . . . . . P—Q4!)

This move is wrong on two counts. In the first place, it blocks the development of White's King Bishop. Secondly, it gives the Knight an inadequate command of the centre. Note that 2 Kt—KB3! is far superior: it does not block the Bishop, and it gives the Knight a more aggressive bearing on the centre.

White's dubious 3 P—B3 has deprived White of the possibility of playing his Queen Knight to Queen Bishop 3. Black alertly reacts with 3 . . . . . . P—Q4; for if White captures this Pawn, Black replies 4 . . . . . . Q×P and White is unable to menace the Queen with 5 Kt—B3.

Guard Your King

The recommendation to play out your pieces rapidly does not apply to the King, of course. As the whole fate of the game depends on the welfare of this piece, he should be kept as far as possible from the thick of the fight. One of the important reasons for developing your King Knight and King Bishop rapidly is to make room for castling. This tucks the King away at the side of the board and removes him from the centre, the scene of intense activity. Many games are lost for failure to follow this all-important rule.

In Diagrams 107 and 108 we see startling retributions follow after careless exposure of the King to decisive attack.

54

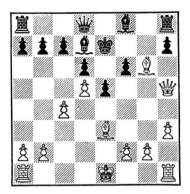

107. *The harried King.*

White to move.

WHITE	BLACK
1 Q×KPch!!	......

It is mate next move, for on 1 ...... BP×Q White has 2 B—Kt5 mate; and on 1 ...... QP×Q there follows 2 B—QB5 mate.

108. *A fatal double check.*

Black to move.

WHITE	BLACK
1	Kt×Q

Black has nothing better, as White's Queen is giving check.

2 Kt—B6 mate

A brutal double check.

Other Opening Pointers

The way you play the opening will determine the kind of prospects you will have later on. If you strive for control of the centre and further your development and get your King into a safe haven, you will have a promising situation for the middle game.

On the other hand, if you ignore the centre, play a whole series of inconclusive Pawn moves, delay the development of your pieces, and leave your King exposed to attack, you are just as surely headed for serious trouble.

Here, then, are a few more simple rules for playing the opening properly. They are easy to apply, yet they can prove immensely valuable.

Inexperienced players are prone to waste time in the opening to snatch insignificant Pawns. The time lost may outweigh by far the value of the Pawn in question. It is therefore a good idea to resist temptation firmly and continue the steady development of your pieces.

Two related faults are attacking prematurely and developing the Queen too soon. This is tempting because of the Queen's enormous powers. But there is also a drawback, precisely because the Queen is so valuable. She can be harried by hostile units of lesser value and must then beat a hasty retreat.

Similarly, premature attacks—usually with the Queen in the forefront—are likely to recoil on the attacker, resulting in considerable loss of time, and sometimes of material as well. Every player has had the experience of succeeding with an unsound attack against weak opposition; but this is clearly something that cannot be recommended in a book!

Finally, avoid the creation of weak points in your position. The most common sin in this respect is optimistically advancing your Pawns beyond the fourth rank in order to drive away enemy pieces. Such advances must be weighed very carefully. Remember that a Pawn once advanced cannot retreat; balance the present good against the potential weakness.

Some Recommended Openings

There are many openings with innumerable variations that branch off into thousands of possibilities. The inexperienced player who tries to memorize a few of them finds that he cannot remember them, or that he fails to apply them correctly, or that his opponent avoids playing "by the book".

Fortunately, there is no need for you to make such frustrating attempts to learn the openings. A small repertoire of standard openings will spare you many pitfalls. Here are two standard openings that will help to solve difficulties in this department.

The first of these is the *Giuoco Piano*—this is Italian for "the quiet game". It proceeds in a placid fashion that makes it easy for you to develop your pieces with a minimum of difficulty.

	WHITE	BLACK
1	P—K4	P—K4

This advance of the King Pawns, you will recall, has been strongly recommended.

	WHITE	BLACK
2	Kt—KB3	. . .

The best development of this Knight—strong action in the centre, coupled with gain of time by attacking Black's King Pawn.

	WHITE	BLACK
2	. . .	Kt—QB3

Another excellent developing move which guards Black's King Pawn.

	WHITE	BLACK
3	B—B4	B—B4

56

Each of these Bishops is on an effective diagonal, bearing down on the King Bishop Pawn. This Pawn is often vulnerable before castling has taken place.

4   P—Q3   . . .

This opens the diagonal for White's Queen Bishop.

4   . . .   Kt—B3

The recommended development for this Knight.

5   B—K3   . . .

The idea is that if Black plays . . . B×B, White has an open King Bishop file after the recapture P×B.

5   . . .   B—Kt3

A strategic retreat: if White plays B×B, Black replies . . . RP×B with an open Queen Rook file.

6   Kt—B3   . . .

White consistently continues his development.

6   . . .   P—Q3

Black opens his Queen Bishop's diagonal.

7   Q—Q2   . . .

White reserves the possibility of castling on either wing.

7   . . .   B—K3
8   B—Kt3   . . .

These Bishop moves have the same ideas behind them as White's and Black's fifth moves. We now have the situation of Diagram 109.

109. *Giuoco Piano.*

Black to move. The position is even. Both players have pursued their development efficiently without wasting any time. At this point Black will castle and White will follow his example.

Another useful opening for adoption by inexperienced players is the *Scotch Opening*, which starts with these moves:

	WHITE	BLACK
1	P—K4	P—K4
2	Kt—KB3	Kt—QB3
3	P—Q4	. . .

This takes up the fight for control of the centre. It also opens up the position for White's pieces. For example, White's Queen Bishop is now ready to come into the game.

3	. . .	P×P
4	Kt×P	B—B4

A perfectly acceptable alternative is 4 . . . Kt—B3 (attacking White's King Pawn), which White can answer with 5 Kt—B3 with even chances.

110. *Scotch Opening.*

White to move. Black threatens to win a piece by capturing White's Knight on the Queen 4 square. White defends most efficiently by developing another piece: 5 B—K3. Generally speaking, the Scotch Opening leads to a livelier game than the Giuoco Piano.

By following the maxims given here and by adopting the Giuoco Piano and Scotch Opening, inexperienced players will find that they can readily hold their own with players of their own class. Later on, as they gain in experience and knowledge, they will want to broaden their knowledge of opening play.

5. BASIC CHECKMATES

The basic checkmates are just that: *basic*. These are the fundamental methods of winning a game with a large material advantage. It sounds easy and it is easy; but to the surprisingly large number of players who are not familiar with these methods, winning a won game can be a very arduous and sometimes impossible task.

Checkmate with the Queen

This is the easiest checkmate—naturally enough, in view of the Queen's enormous powers. The checkmating procedure is illustrated in Diagrams 111 and 112

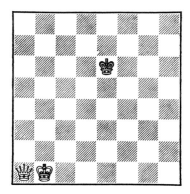

111. *King and Queen* vs. *King.*

White to move.

	WHITE	BLACK
1	K—B2	K—Q4
2	K—Q3	K—B4
3	Q—B6!	K—Q4
4	Q—K7!	K—B3
5	K—B4	K—Kt3
6	Q—Q7!	K—R3
7	K—B5	K—R4
8	Q—QR7 mate	

See Diagram 112 for the final position.

112. *Checkmate by the Queen.*

The outstandingly important move in this procedure is a long-range Queen move that enormously cuts down the hostile King's mobility. (In this case the move was 3 Q—B6!) Meanwhile the White King approaches as well, and the harmonious co-operation of King and Queen forces the lone King to a side row, where check can then be administered.

59

Checkmate with the Rook

This mate takes a little longer than the Queen checkmate because the Rook lacks diagonal powers. However, the process is still rather easy. See Diagrams 113 and 114.

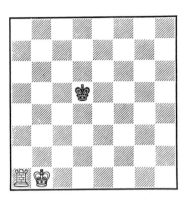

113. *King and Rook* vs. *King.*

114. *Checkmate by the Rook.*

White to move.

WHITE	BLACK
1 K—Kt2	K—Q5
2 K—B2	K—K5
3 K—B3	K—K4
4 K—B4	K—K5
5 R—K1ch!	K—B4
6 K—Q4	K—B5
7 R—KB1ch!	K—Kt4
8 K—K4	K—Kt3
9 K—K5	K—Kt4
10 R—KKt1ch!	K—R4
11 K—B4	K—R3
12 K—B5	K—R2
13 K—B6	K—R1
14 K—B7	K—R2
15 R—R1 mate	

Note the position of the Kings, directly facing each other, with the Black King trapped on a side row. The technique of forcing the Black King back to the last row is very instructive. The key move here is 5 R—K1ch!, played at a point where the two Kings face each other, so that the Black King is forced to give way. (The process is repeated at White's seventh and tenth move.) Master this principle and you will find that the Rook checkmate is child's play.

Checkmate with the Two Bishops

A single Bishop, as we know, cannot give checkmate; but two Bishops can do so. The process should take about 17 moves at most from the least favourable position—one in which the lone King is in the centre of the board, and the stronger side's King is far away. To shorten the process somewhat, we start the mating process from a more favourable position. In any event, the underlying idea remains the same: the lone King must be forced to a corner square. See Diagrams 115 and 116.

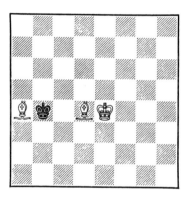

115. *King and two Bishops* vs. *King.*

White to move.

	WHITE	BLACK
1	B—Q1	K—B5
2	B—QB2	K—Kt5
3	K—Q5	K—Kt4
4	B—QB5!	K—R3
5	K—B6	K—R4
6	B—Q6	K—R3
7	B—Kt4	K—R2
8	K—B7	K—R3
9	B—Q3ch	K—R2
10	B—QB5ch	K—R1
11	B—K4 mate	

116. *Checkmate by the two Bishops.*

As you have noticed, this process requires the closest kind of co-operation between the Bishops and their King. The significant moves here are 3 K—Q5! and 4 B—QB5! Each of these moves plays an essential role in cutting down the mobility of the lone King. Only by eliminating the lone King's access to certain squares can he be forced to the side and then to a corner square.

Checkmate with Bishop and Knight

This mate requires more moves than the mate with the two Bishops. But it is highly rewarding because it calls for first-class co-operation on the part of the checkmating pieces. The checkmate can only be effected by driving the lone King to a corner square. In addition, this corner square must be of the same colour as the one that the Bishop travels on. If your Bishop moves on white squares, for example, the lone King will be checkmated on a white corner square.

The checkmate process is illustrated in Diagrams 117 to 119. The ending is presented here in a somewhat advanced stage, after the lone King has been driven to a side row. You are now familiar with the technique for accomplishing this—systematically cutting down the lone King's access to squares and gradually forcing him back.

117. *King and Bishop and Knight* vs. *King.*

White to move.

	WHITE	BLACK	
1	K—B6	K—R1	
2	Kt—B7ch	K—Kt1	
3	B—B5	K—B1	
4	B—R7!	K—K1	
5	Kt—K5!	K—B1	
6	Kt—Q7ch	K—K1	
7	K—K6	K—Q1	
8	K—Q6	K—K1	
9	B—Kt6ch!	K—Q1	
10	B—R5	K—B1	See Diagram 118.

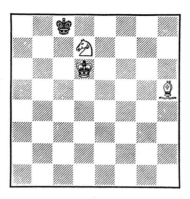

118. *White has made considerable progress toward the white corner square.*

11	Kt—B5!	K—Q1
12	Kt—Kt7ch	K—B1
13	K—B6	K—Kt1
14	K—Kt6	K—B1
15	B—Kt4ch	K—Kt1
16	B—B5	K—R1

Now the end is very near.

17	Kt—B5	K—Kt1
18	Kt—R6ch	K—R1
19	B—K4 mate	

See Diagram 119.

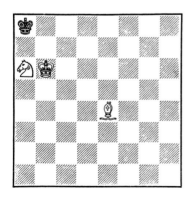

119. *Checkmate by Bishop and Knight.*

This is the basic checkmate which calls for the most sustained effort and the most harmonious co-operation of all three checkmating pieces. It is an excellent ending to practise because it gives such a good idea of how the pieces work together.

6. THE ENDGAME

The endgame, as its name indicates, is the final stage of the game. It is highly simplified, with most of the pieces gone; the Queens are rarely left on the board. Precisely because the position is so simplified, this is the stage in which a player has the best chance of turning a material advantage to account; the prospective loser has comparatively little chance to affect the issue by trying to introduce complications.

It is one of the great weaknesses of average players that they underestimate the importance of the endgame. Ability to play this phase of the game well can become one of your most valuable assets. By studying the standard endings in this section you can create many favourable opportunities for winning.

The average player can enormously increase his endgame skill and the number of his victories if he comes to realize that the most important phase of endgame play revolves about the promotion of a Pawn. For the successful queening of a Pawn gives him a whole Queen ahead, enabling him to deliver checkmate (Diagrams 111 and 112) without the slightest trouble. It is at this point that we can appreciate the fact that the "lowly" Pawn is a pearl of great price.

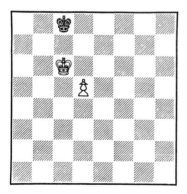

120. *Basic King and Pawn ending.*

White to move.

WHITE	BLACK
1 P—Q6	K—Q1
2 P—Q7	K—K2
3 K—B7 and wins	

White continues 4 P—Q8/Q and then proceeds to force checkmate.

64

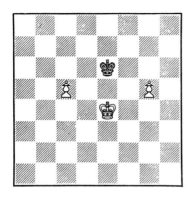

121. *The power of passed Pawns.*

White to move. White has two passed Pawns—there are no hostile Pawns to stop their advance. In fact, White wins without his King's help.

	WHITE	BLACK
1	P—Kt6	K—B3
2	P—B6	K—K3
3	P—Kt7	K—B2
4	P—B7 and wins	

122. *The distant passed Pawn.*

White to move. His Rook Pawn, the distant passed Pawn, cannot be stopped.

	WHITE	BLACK
1	P—R4	K—B1
2	P—R5	K—K1
3	P—R6	K—Q1
4	P—R7 and wins	

Black's King was too far away from the critical sector.

123. *The power of the distant passed Pawn.*

124. *White must preserve his Pawn!*

See Diagram 123

White to move.

WHITE	BLACK
1 P—R5!	K—B3
2 K—K5!	K—Kt4
3 K—B6	K×P
4 K×KtP	K—Kt3
5 K×P	K—B3
6 K—K6	K—B2
7 K—K7!	K—B1
8 P—B5 and wins	

Black's King was drawn off to the Queen-side, leaving his Pawns defenceless. This illustrates the power of the distant passed Pawn.

125. *A neat trick.*

White to move.

WHITE	BLACK
1 R—KR8!	R×P

Otherwise White queens his Pawn.
2 R—R7ch and wins

Black's Rook is lost. This stratagem turns up fairly frequently in Rook and Pawn endings. It is sometimes called the "X-ray" attack.

See Diagram 124

White to move.

WHITE	BLACK
1 B—B4!	P—Q4

If 1 . . . K—B2; 2 P—B5! wins.

2 P—B5!	. . .

Here 2 P×P?? draws.

2 . . .	K—R3
3 K—Q4	K—Kt4
4 B—K3!	K—Kt5
5 K—K5!	K—B5
6 K—Q6	K—Kt4
7 B—B2	K—R3
8 K×BP and wins	

White will queen his Pawn.

126. *A standard Rook and Pawn ending.*

White to move.

WHITE	BLACK
1 R—Q1ch!	K—B2
2 R—Q4!	R—Kt8
3 K—K7	R—K8ch
4 K—B6	R—KB8ch
5 K—K6	R—K8ch
6 K—B5	R—KB8ch
7 R—KB4 and wins	

The Pawn must queen. 1 R—Q1ch! drives Black's King away.

7. SALVAGING LOST ENDGAMES

Quite naturally we all concentrate on winning. But it is also important to be able to snatch a draw from a lost game. Indeed, our relief and gratification at such a last-minute rescue make up one of the most enjoyable aspects of chess.

As it happens, there are quite a few valuable standard positions in which it is possible to stave off defeat—in some cases, with a Queen down! Here are some of the more common ones (Diagrams 127 to 134).

127. *Only a draw.*

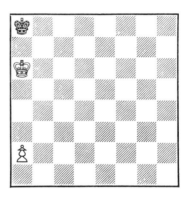

128. *White cannot win.*

White to move.

	WHITE	BLACK
1	P—Q7ch	K—Q1
2	K—Q6	Drawn

Black is stalemated. White had no choice at move 2, as he had to keep his Pawn protected. With Black to move in the diagram position, White wins. See Diagram 120.

White to move.

	WHITE	BLACK
1	K—Kt6	K—Kt1
2	P—R4	K—R1
3	P—R5	K—Kt1
4	P—R6	K—R1
5	P—R7	Drawn

Black is stalemated. The Rook Pawn can never win if the hostile King is at or near his Rook 1.

There are some cases in which a Rook Pawn does not win even when supported by a Bishop. In Diagram 129 White wins because his Bishop commands the queening square. In Diagram 130 White cannot win because his Bishop does not command the queening square.

129. *White wins.*

130. *White draws.*

White to move.

WHITE	BLACK
1 B—Q5ch	K—Kt1
2 P—R7ch	K—B1
3 P—R8/Qch and wins

White will checkmate very shortly. In Diagram 130, however, White's Bishop is on the wrong colour.

White to move.

WHITE	BLACK
1 K—R5	K—R2
2 K—Kt5	K—R1
3 K—Kt6	K—Kt1
4 B—K5ch	K—R1!

Drawn. Any effort to win will only stalemate Black; for example, 5 P—R7.

The advantage of an extra Pawn in Bishop and Pawn endings and Rook and Pawn endings is generally decisive. Yet there are exceptions, and two of these are shown in Diagrams 131 and 132.

131. *Bishops on opposite colours.*

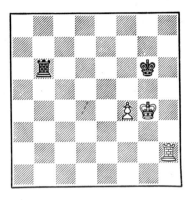

132. *White cannot win.*

It does not matter who moves first here. When one Bishop moves on white squares and the other on black, the win often becomes impossible even where a player is two Pawns to the good. This applies particularly to the above position, where the Pawns ought to be on *black* squares. As matters stand, White can never play P—B6ch because Black's Bishop is an efficient blockader. If White had a Bishop on black squares he would win rather easily.

Black to move.

	WHITE	BLACK
1	. . .	K—Kt2
2	K—Kt5	R—QB3
3	P—B5	R—QKt3
4	R—QR2	R—Q3
5	R—R7ch	K—Kt1
6	P—B6	R—Q8!
7	K—Kt6	R—KKt8ch
8	K—B5	K—B1
9	K—K6	R—K8ch
10	K—B5	K—Kt1

Drawn. White can make no headway.

It verges on the incredible that a player can draw with only a Pawn against a Queen. Yet there are certain typical situations in which this happens. They are shown in Diagrams 133 and 134.

133. *Black draws.*

White to move. To stop the Pawn from queening, he must check.

WHITE	BLACK
1 Q—KKt3ch	K—R8

White cannot win. If he makes a Queen move to relieve the stalemate position, Black moves his King, again threatening to queen.

134. *Black draws.*

Black to move. The right drawing method is to play the King into the corner.

WHITE	BLACK
1 . . .	K—R8!

Now Black threatens to queen the Pawn. If White replies 2 Q×P, Black is stalemated. No check will accomplish anything.

From your study of these remarkable positions, you have learned how it is possible on occasion to extract a creditable and satisfying draw from what seems a hopelessly lost game. The knowledge thus gained should be of use to you time and again in your own games.

8. INSTRUCTIVE GAMES

There are several good reasons for studying these games carefully. One is that if you have never played a game these brief encounters will give you the feel of an actual game. Another valuable aspect of the games is that they illustrate common faults and show you how drastically these faults can be punished. Finally, these examples teach an important lesson in showing how quickly a game of chess can be won—or lost.

Centre Game

	WHITE	BLACK
1	P—K4	P—K4
2	P—Q4	. . .

Theoretically this advance in the centre is commendable, but it has the drawback of leading to a loss of time. The previously recommended 2 Kt—KB3 is better.

2	. . .	P×P
3	Q×P	. . .

White's Queen comes into play prematurely and is at once exposed to attack.

3	. . .	Kt—QB3!

This is the move that spoils the opening for White.

71

135. *Black gains time.*

White to move. Black's Queen Knight attacks the White Queen, forcing White to lose a move in bringing the Queen to a safe post.

    4 Q—K3   Kt—B3

Already Black is distinctly ahead in development.

    5 B—B4   Kt—K4

Generally speaking, you are better off not to move the same piece more than once in the opening. However, since the move is bound up with a threat (. . . Kt×B), the principle can be waived here.

136. *White's King Bishop is attacked.*

White to move. Though Black has violated opening
theory by moving his Knight twice, he is gaining time
by attacking White's Bishop. Also, he is laying the
groundwork for a very subtle trap.

6 B—Kt3   B—Kt5ch

A very tricky move. White would be well advised to counter this check with a
developing move, say 7 Kt—QB3 or perhaps 7 B—Q2.

7 P—QB3   . . .

This interposition is not fatal, but it is certainly questionable. Note that White's
Queen Bishop Pawn no longer controls White's Queen 3 square. This is a very
important factor in the coming play.

7 . . .   B—B4!

E*

137. *Danger signal for White.*
White to move. If White captures the unprotected
Bishop with his Queen, Black replies . . . Kt—Q6ch
forking the White King and Queen.

In the face of Black's insidious Knight fork menace, White must beat a prudent
retreat with his Queen. The question is, where? For example, 8 Q—B4?? would
not do because of 8 . . . Kt—Q6ch still winning by means of the Knight fork.

    8 Q—Kt3??   . . .

A mistake, although it must be admitted that Black's startling refutation was
not easy to foresee.

White's best was 8 Q—K2, although it would have meant that White had taken
three moves to get to a square that could have been reached in *one* move with proper
play.

    8 . . .   B×Pch!!
    Resigns

138. *Why does White resign?*

White to move. White must capture the Bishop because there is a double attack on his King and Queen. If White captures the Bishop with his Queen, Black replies 9 . . . Kt—Q6ch. If White captures the Bishop with his King, Black replies 9 . . . Kt×Pch. In either case, Black wins the White Queen with a Knight forking check and further resistance is hopeless. So White prefers to resign.

Beware of Thoughtless Development

We have just seen an example of indiscriminate development. This is a fault which almost automatically brings its own punishment. Overleaf is another example of the same theme:

ALEKHINE'S DEFENCE

WHITE	BLACK
1 P—K4	Kt—KB3

This unconventional Knight development has the virtue of developing the Knight toward the centre. Yet its consequences can be very tricky. It is therefore best left to highly experienced players.

139. *Black's Knight move is provocative.*

White to move. He decides to drive off the Knight, at the possible risk of weakening his Pawns by unduly optimistic advances.

2 P—K5	Kt—Q4
3 P—QB4	. . .

140. *The Knight is driven to an unfavourable square.*

Black to move. Black's Knight is driven away from the centre. On the other hand, White's Pawn moves are contributing nothing to his development. So far, the disadvantages cancel each other.

    3 . . .   Kt—Kt3
    4 P—Q4   . . .

Still another Pawn move, but this one has the virtue of opening the White Queen Bishop's diagonal and supporting his advanced King Pawn.

Black's indicated reply is 4 . . . P—Q3, putting some restraint on the White Pawns and opening up the diagonal of his Queen Bishop. Instead, he commits a frightful blunder.

    4 . . .   Kt—B3 ? ?

Unbelievable as it may seem, Black is now forced to lose a piece, no matter how he plays.

    5 P—Q5!   . . .

This surprise move wins a piece against any play by Black.

141. *Black is left without a good reply.*

Black to move. The apparently safe 5 . . . Kt—Kt1 will not do because of 6 P—B5 and the unfortunate Knight has no retreat. On the other hand, if Black tries 5 . . . Kt—Kt5 White still wins a piece with 6 P—B5! forcing 6 . . . Kt/Kt3 × P, whereupon 7 P—QR3 compels Black to lose one of the Knights.

           5 . . .   Kt × KP

On the face of it, this is an easy way out. But Black is lost just the same.

           6 P—B5   Kt/Kt3—B5

Black's Knights are vulnerable.

           7 P—B4!   . . .

142. *One of Black's Knights is lost.*

Black to move. If his attacked Knight retreats, White can simply reply 8 B×Kt with a piece to the good. Black resigned a few moves later. The rest of the game does not concern us.

Watch for Hostile Threats

There is no surer way to lose than by ignoring your opponent's threats. That is why you must ask yourself after every move by your opponent, "What's he up to? What does he threaten? Can he capture any of my forces?" The following brief game shows what can happen when this self-questioning process is ignored.

FRENCH DEFENCE

WHITE	BLACK
1 P—K4	P—K3

A change from the openings we have seen so far. Instead of replying . . . P—K4, Black prefers to prepare to dispute the centre by 2 . . . P—Q4. This is an acceptable method, if Black bears in mind that his Queen Bishop may be somewhat lacking in mobility.

2 P—Q4	P—Q4
3 P—K5	. . .

143. *White strives for "encirclement".*

Black to move. The presence of White's King Pawn on King 5 has a very cramping effect on Black's development.

For example, he is unable to play . . . Kt—KB3—the best development for his King Knight.

3 . . .   P—QB4!

Excellent. By trying to remove White's Queen Pawn (which supports White's King Pawn), Black has taken the first step towards freedom.

4 Q—Kt4?!   . . .

Another move about which we have mixed feelings. One must always be suspicious about an early development of the Queen, as she is often exposed to attack in such situations (see Diagram 135). On the other hand, the Queen move is consistent with White's master plan—cramping Black's game. In this case, Black is unable to develop his King Bishop—at least for the time being.

4 . . .   P×P

Black carries out his strategic plan consistently—first he removes White's Queen Pawn, so that he can concentrate on his King Pawn. Also he hopes for 5 Q×QP, which he will answer with 5 . . . Kt—QB3! gaining valuable time.

5 Kt—KB3   . . .

White refuses to lose time with repeated Queen moves.

5 . . .   P—B4

Black attacks the White Queen, but at the cost of weakening his King's position and depriving himself of the opportunity of ridding himself subsequently of the burdensome hostile King Pawn with . . . P—B3.

Black had a better course in 5 . . . Kt—QB3 followed by . . . KKt—K2 and then . . . Kt—Kt3. In this way Black would have been well on the way to carrying out his development in an orderly fashion and at the same time he would have a strong counter-attack on White's King Pawn.

6 Q-Kt3   Kt—QB3

7 B—K2   . . .

144. *Black must be alert.*

Black to move. White's quiet development of his King Bishop is bound up with a subtle trap that Black completely misses. Had he realized his opponent's devilish design he would have played 7 . . . Q—Kt3 or 7 . . . Q—B2.

7 . . .   B—Q2?

Black innocently misses the point, playing just the very move that makes White's trap work.

8 Kt×P!!   . . .

145. *What does White have in mind?*
Black to move. Here is what White hopes for:

	WHITE	BLACK
8	. . .	Kt × Kt ? ?
9	B—R5ch	P—KKt3
10	Q × Pch!!	P × Q
11	B × Pch	K—K2
12	B—Kt5ch	Kt—B3
13	B × Kt mate!	

But this is only an imaginary continuation, so let us go back to the position of Diagram 145 and see what happens in the actual game.

8   . . .   Kt × Kt ? ?

He captures the Knight after all. By declining the Knight and playing some reasonable move such as 8 . . . Q—Kt3, he would still have had a game of sorts.

9 B—R5ch   . . .

So far the game has proceeded as in our hypothetical continuation. But now Black varies, as he realizes that 9 . . . P—KKt3 must lose.

9 . . .   K—K2

Black reckons smugly on 10 B—Kt5ch, Kt—KB3; 11 P×Ktch, P×P when he threatens . . . P×B as well as . . . Kt×Pch winning White's Queen Rook. But he gets a rude jolt.

10 Q—QR3 mate!

146. An aeroplane check.
Black has been checkmated by a remarkable Queen
move. This completes the punishment inflicted on him
for his failure to see through White's plans.

You now have all the information you need to play chess with enjoyment against players of your own class. If you want to improve you will need further study; your further progress will be determined by your own choice.